ON THE TRANQUILITY OF THE MIND

Seneca

Translated by Aubrey Stewart in 1900.

SERENUS: When I made examination of myself, it became evident, Seneca, that some of my vices are uncovered and displayed so openly that I can put my hand upon them, some are more hidden and lurk in a corner, some are not always present but recur at intervals; and I should say that the last are by far the most troublesome, being like roving enemies that spring upon one when the opportunity offers, and allow one neither to be ready as in war, nor to be off guard as in peace.

Nevertheless the state in which I find myself most of all — for why should I not admit the truth to you as to a physician? — is that I have neither been honestly set free from the things that I hated and feared, nor, on the other hand, am I in bondage to them; while the condition in which I am placed is not the worst, yet I am complaining and fretful — I am neither sick nor well. There is no need for you to say that all the virtues are weakly at the beginning, that firmness and strength are added by time. I am well aware also that the virtues that struggle for outward show, I mean for position and the fame of eloquence and all that comes under the verdict of others, do grow stronger as time passes — both those that provide real strength and those that trick us out with a sort of dye with a view to pleasing, must wait long years until gradually length of time develops color — but I greatly fear that habit, which brings stability to most things, may cause this fault of mine to become more deeply implanted. Of things evil as well as good long intercourse induces love.

The nature of this weakness of mind that halts between two things and inclines strongly neither to the right nor to the wrong, I cannot show you so well all at once as a part at a time; I shall tell you what befalls me — you will find a name for my malady. I am possessed by the very greatest love of frugality, I must confess; I do not like a couch made up for display, nor clothing brought forth from a chest or pressed by weights and a thousand mangles to make it glossy, but homely and cheap, that is neither preserved nor to be put on with anxious care; the food that I like is neither prepared nor watched by a household of slaves, it does not need to be ordered many days before nor to be served by many hands, but is easy to get and abundant; there is nothing far-fetched or costly about it, nowhere will there be any lack of it, it is burdensome neither to the purse nor to the body, nor will it return by the way it entered; the servant that I like is a young home-born slave without training or skill; the silver is my country-bred father's heavy plate bearing no stamp of the maker's name, and the table is not notable for the variety of its markings or known to the town from the many fashionable owners through whose hands it has passed, but one that stands for use, and will neither cause the eyes of any guest to linger upon it with pleasure nor fire them with envy.

Then, after all these things have had my full approval, my mind is dazzled by the magnificence of some training-school for pages, by the sight of slaves bedecked with gold and more carefully arrayed than the leaders of a public procession, and a whole regiment of glittering attendants; by the sight of a house where one even treads on precious stones and riches are scattered about in every corner, where the very roofs glitter, and the whole town pays court and escorts an inheritance on the road to ruin. And what shall I say of the waters, transparent to the bottom, that flow around the guests even as they banquet, what of the feasts that are worthy of their setting? Coming from a long abandonment to thrift, luxury has poured around me the wealth of its splendor, and echoed around me, on every side. My sight falters a little, for I can lift up my heart towards it more easily than my eyes. And so I come back, not worse, but sadder, and I do not walk among my paltry possessions with head erect as before, and there enters a secret sting and the doubt whether the other life is not better. None of these things changes me, yet none of them fails to disturb me.

I resolve to obey the commands of my teachers and plunge into the midst of public life; I resolve to try to gain office and the consulship, attracted of course, not by the purple or by the lictor's rods, but by the desire to be more serviceable and useful to my friends and relatives and all my countrymen and then to all mankind. Ready and determined, I follow Zeno, Cleanthes, and Chrysippus, of whom none the less not one entered upon public life, and not one failed to urge others to do so. And then, whenever something upsets my mind, which is unused to meeting shocks, whenever something happens that is either unworthy of me, and many such occur in the lives of all human beings, or that does not proceed very easily, or when things that are not to be accounted of great value demand much of my time, I turn back to my leisure, and just as wearied flocks too do, I quicken my pace towards home.

I resolve to confine my life within its own walls: "Let no one," I say, "who will make me no worthy return for such a loss rob me of a single day; let my mind be fixed upon itself, let it cultivate itself, let it busy itself with nothing outside, nothing that looks towards an umpire; let it love the tranquillity that is remote from public and private concern." But when my mind has been aroused by reading of great bravery, and noble examples have applied the spur, I want to rush into the forum, to lend my voice to one man; to offer such assistance to another as, even if it will not help, will be an effort to help; or to check the pride of someone in the forum who has been unfortunately puffed up by his successes.

And in my literary studies I think that it is surely better to fix my eye on the theme itself, and, keeping this uppermost when I speak, to trust meanwhile to the theme to supply the words so that unstudied language may follow it wherever it leads. I say: "What need is there to compose something that will last for centuries? Will you not give up striving to keep posterity from being silent about you? You were born for death; a silent funeral is less troublesome!

"And so to pass the time, write something in simple style, for your own use, not for publication; they that study for the day have less need to labor." Then again, when my mind has been uplifted by the greatness of its thoughts, it becomes ambitious of words, and with higher aspirations it desires higher expression, and language issues forth to match the dignity of the theme: forgetful then of my rule and of my more restrained judgment, I am swept to loftier heights by an utterance that is no longer   my   own.
Not to indulge longer in details, I am in all things attended by this weakness of good intention. In fact I fear that I am gradually losing ground, or, what causes me even more worry, that I am hanging like one who is always on the verge of falling, and that perhaps I am in a more serious condition than I myself perceive; for we take a favorable view of our private matters, and partiality always hampers our judgment.

I fancy that many men would have arrived at wisdom if they had not fancied that they had already arrived, if they had not dissembled about certain traits in their character and passed by others with their eyes shut. For there is no reason for you to suppose that the adulation of other people is more ruinous to us than our own. Who dares to tell himself the truth? Who, though he is surrounded by a horde of applauding sycophants, is not for all that his own greatest flatterer? I beg you, therefore, if you have any remedy by which you could stop this fluctuation of mine, to deem me worthy of being indebted to you for tranquillity. I know that these mental disturbances of mine are not dangerous and give no promise of a storm; to express what I complain of in apt metaphor, I am distressed, not by a tempest, but by sea-sickness.

Do you, then, take from me this trouble, whatever it be, and rush to the rescue of one who is struggling in full sight of land.

SENECA: In truth, Serenus, I have for a long time been silently asking myself to what I should liken such a condition of mind, and I can find nothing that so closely approaches it as the state of those who, after being released from a long and serious illness, are sometimes touched with fits of fever and slight disorders, and, freed from the last traces of them, are nevertheless disquieted with mistrust, and, though now quite well, stretch out their wrist to a physician and complain unjustly of any trace of heat in their body. It is not, Serenus, that these are not quite well in body, but that they are not quite used to being well; just as even a tranquil sea will show some ripple, particularly when it has just subsided after a storm. What you need, therefore, is not any of those harsher measures which we have already left behind, the necessity of opposing yourself at this point, of being angry with yourself at that, of sternly urging yourself on at another, but that which comes last — confidence in yourself and the belief that you are on the right path, and have not been led astray by the many cross-tracks of those who are roaming in every direction, some of whom are wandering very near the path itself. But what you desire is something great and supreme and very near to being a god — to be unshaken.

This abiding stability of mind the Greeks call *euthyimia*, "well-being of the soul," on which there is an excellent treatise by Democritus; I call it tranquillity. For there is no need to imitate and reproduce words in their Greek shape; the thing itself, which is under discussion, must be designated by some name which ought to have, not the form, but the force, of the Greek term. What we are seeking, therefore, is how the mind may always pursue a steady and favorable course, may be well-disposed towards itself, and may view its condition with joy, and suffer no interruption of this joy, but may abide in a peaceful state, being never uplifted nor ever cast down. This will be "tranquillity." Let us seek in a general way how it may be obtained; then from the universal remedy you will appropriate as much as you like. Meanwhile we must drag forth into the light the whole of the infirmity, and each one will then recognize his own share of it; at the same time you will understand how much less trouble you have with your self-depreciation than those who, fettered to some showy declaration and struggling beneath the burden of some grand title, are held more by shame than by desire to the pretence they are making.

All are in the same case, both those, on the one hand, who are plagued with fickleness and boredom and a continual shifting of purpose, and those, on the other other, who loll and yawn. Add also those who, just like the wretches who find it hard to sleep, change their position and settle first in one way and then in another, until finally they find rest through weariness. By repeatedly altering the condition of their life they are at last left in that in which, not the dislike of making a change, but old age, that shrinks from novelty, has caught them. And add also those who by fault, not of firmness of character, but of inertia, are not fickle enough, and live, not as they wish, but as they have begun. The characteristics of the malady are countless in number, but it has only one effect —

to be dissatisfied with oneself. This springs from a lack of mental poise and from timid or unfulfilled desires, when men either do not dare, or do not attain, as much as they desire, and become entirely dependent upon hope; such men are always unstable and changeable, as must necessarily be the fate of those who live in suspense.

They strive to attain their prayers by every means, they teach and force themselves to do dishonorable and difficult things, and, when their effort is without reward, they are tortured by the fruitless disgrace and grieve, not because they wished for what was wrong, but because they wished in vain. Then regret for what they have begun lays hold upon them, and the fear of beginning again, and then creeps in the agitation of a mind which can find no issue, because they can neither rule nor obey their desires, and the hesitancy of a life which fails to find its way clear, and then the dullness of a soul that lies torpid amid abandoned hopes. And all these tendencies are aggravated when from hatred of their laborious ill-success men have taken refuge in leisure and in solitary studies, which are unendurable to a mind that is intent upon public affairs, desirous of action, and naturally restless, because assuredly it has too few resources within itself; when, therefore, the pleasures have been withdrawn which business itself affords to those who are busily engaged, the mind cannot endure home, solitude, and the walls of a room, and sees with dislike that it has been left to itself.

From this comes that boredom and dissatisfaction and the vacillation of a mind that nowhere finds rest, and the sad and languid endurance of one's leisure; especially when one is ashamed to confess the real causes of this condition and bashfullness drives its tortures inward; the desires pent up within narrow bounds, from which there is no escape, strangle one another. Thence comes mourning and melancholy and the thousand waverings of an unsettled mind, which its aspirations hold in suspense and then disappointment renders melancholy. Thence comes that feeling which makes men loathe their own leisure and complain that they themselves have nothing to be busy with; thence too the bitterest jealousy of the advancements of others. For their unhappy sloth fosters envy, and, because they could not succeed themselves, they wish every one else to be ruined; then from this aversion to the progress of others and despair of their own their mind becomes incensed against Fortune, and complains of the times, and retreats into corners and broods over its trouble until it becomes weary and sick of itself.

For it is the nature of the human mind to be active and prone to movement. Welcome to it is every opportunity for excitement and distraction, and still more welcome to all those worst natures which willingly wear themselves out in being employed. Just as there are some sores which crave the hands that will hurt them and rejoice to be touched, and as a foul itch of the body delights in whatever scratches, exactly so, I would say, do these minds upon which, so to speak, desires have broken out like wicked sores find pleasure in toil and vexation. For there are certain things that delight our body also while causing it a sort of pain, as turning over and changing a side that is not yet tired and taking one position after another to get cool. Homer's hero Achilles is like that — lying now on his face, now on his back, placing himself in various attitudes, and, just as sick men do, enduring nothing very long and using changes as remedies.

Hence men undertake wide-ranging travel, and wander over remote shores, and their fickleness, always discontented with the present, gives proof of itself now on land and now on sea. "Now let us head for Campania," they say. And now when soft living palls, "Let us see the wild parts," they say, "let us hunt out the passes of Bruttium and Lucania." And yet amid that wilderness something is missing — something pleasant wherein their pampered eyes may find relief from the lasting squalor of those rugged regions: "Let us head for Tarentum with its famous harbor and its mild winter climate, and a territory rich enough to have a horde of people even in antiquity." Too long have their ears missed the shouts and the din; it delights them by now even to enjoy human blood: "Let us now turn our course toward the city." They undertake one journey after another and change spectacle for spectacle. As Lucretius says:

Thus ever from himself doth each man flee.

But what does he gain if he does not escape from himself? He ever follows himself and weighs upon himself as his own most burdensome companion. And so we ought to understand that what we struggle with is the fault, not of the places, but of ourselves; when there is need of endurance, we are weak, and we cannot bear toil or pleasure or ourselves or anything very long. It is this that has driven some men to death, because by often altering their purpose they were always brought back to the same things and had left themselves no room tor anything new. They began to be sick of life and the world itself, and from the self-indulgences that wasted them was born the thought: "How long shall I endure the same things?"

You ask what help, in my opinion, should be employed to overcome this tedium. The best course would be, as Athenodorus says, to occupy oneself with practical matters, the management of public affairs, and the duties of a citizen. For as some men pass the day in seeking the sun and in exercise and care of the body, and as athletes find it is most profitable by far to devote the greater part of the day to the development of their muscles and the strength to which alone they have dedicated themselves; so for you, who are training your mind for the struggle of political life, by far the most desirable thing is to be busy at one task. For, whenever a man has the set purpose to make himself useful to his countrymen and all mortals, he both gets practice and does service at the same time when he has placed himself in the very midst of active duties, serving to the best of his ability the interests both of the public and of the individual.

"But because," he continues, "in this mad world of ambition where chicanery so frequently twists right into wrong, simplicity is hardly safe, and is always sure to meet with more that hinders than helps it, we ought indeed to withdraw from the forum and public life, but a great mind has an opportunity to display itself freely even in private life; nor, just as the activity of lions and animals is restrained by their dens, is it so of man's, whose greatest achievements are wrought in retirement. Let a man, however, hide himself away bearing in mind that, wherever be secretes his leisure, he should be willing to benefit the individual man and mankind by his intellect, his voice, and his counsel. For the man that does good service to the state is not merely he who brings forward candidates and defends the accused and votes for peace and war, but he also who admonishes young men, who instills virtue into their minds, supplying the great lack of good teachers, who lays hold upon those that are rushing wildly in pursuit of money and luxury, and draws them back, and, if he accomplishes nothing else, at least retards them — such a man performs a public service even in private life.

"Or does he accomplish more who in the office of praetor, whether in cases between citizens and foreigners or in cases between citizens, delivers to suitors the verdict his assistant has formulated, than he who teaches the meaning of justice, of piety, of endurance, of bravery, of contempt of death, of knowledge of the gods, and how secure and free is the blessing of a good conscience? If, then, the time that you have stolen from public duties is bestowed upon studies, you will neither have deserted, nor refused, your office. For a soldier is not merely one who stands in line and defends the right or the left wing, but he also who guards the gates and fills, not an idle, but a less dangerous, post, who keeps watch at night and has charge of the armory; these offices, though they are bloodless, yet count as military service. If you devote yourself to studies, you will have escaped all your disgust at life, you will not long for night to come because you are weary of the light, nor will you be either burdensome to yourself or useless to others; you will attract many to friendship and those that gather about you will be the most excellent.

"For virtue, though obscured, is never concealed, but always gives signs of its presence; whoever is worthy will trace her out by her footsteps. But if we give up society altogether and, turning our back upon the human race, live with our thoughts fixed only upon ourselves, this solitude deprived of every interest will be followed by a want of something to be accomplished. We shall begin to put up some buildings, to pull down others, to thrust back the sea, to cause waters to flow despite the obstacles of nature, and shall make ill disposition of the time which Nature has given us to be used.

"Some use it sparingly, others wastefully; some of us spend it in such a way that we are able to give an account of it, others in such a way — and nothing can be more shameful — that we have no balance left. Often a man who is very old in years has no evidence to prove that he has lived a long time other than his age."

To me, my dearest Serenus, Athenodorus seems to have surrendered too quickly to the times, to have retreated too quickly. I myself would not deny that sometimes one must retire, but it should be a gradual retreat without surrendering the standards, without surrendering the honor of a soldier; those are more respected by their enemies and safer who come to terms with their arms in their hands. This is what I think Virtue and Virtue's devotee should do. If Fortune shall get the upper hand and shall cut off the opportunity for action, let a man not straightway turn his back and flee, throwing away his arms and seeking some hiding-place, as if there were anywhere a place where Fortune could not reach him, but let him devote himself to his duties more sparingly, and, after making choice, let him find something in which he may be useful to the state.

Is he not permitted to be a soldier? Let him seek public office. Must he live in a private station? Let him be a pleader. Is he condemned to silence? Let him help his countrymen by his silent support. Is it dangerous even to enter the forum? In private houses, at the public spectacles, at feasts let him show himself a good comrade, a faithful friend, a temperate feaster. Has he lost the duties of a citizen? Let him exercise those of a man. The very reason for our magnanimity in not shutting ourselves up within the walls of one city, in going forth into intercourse with the whole earth, and in claiming the world as our country, was that we might have a wider field for our virtue. Is the tribunal closed to you, and are you barred from the rostrum and the hustings? Look how many broad stretching countries lie open behind you, how many peoples; never can you be blocked from any part so large that a still larger will not be left to you.

But take care that this is not wholly your own fault; you are not willing to serve the state except as a consul or prytanis or herald or sufete. What if you should be unwilling to serve in the army except as a general or a tribune? Even if others shall hold the front line and your lot has placed you among those of the third line, from there where you are do service with your voice, encouragement, example, and spirit; even though a man's hands are cut off, he finds that he can do something for his side in battle if he stands his ground and helps with the shouting. Some such thing is what you should do. If Fortune has removed you from the foremost position in the state, you should, nevertheless, stand your ground and help with the shouting, and if someone stops your throat, you should, nevertheless, stand your ground and help in silence.

The service of a good citizen is never useless; by being heard and seen, by his expression, by his gesture, by his silent stubbornness, and by his very walk he helps. As there are certain salutary things that without our tasting and touching them benefit us by their mere odor, so virtue sheds her advantage even from a distance, and in hiding.

Whether she walks abroad and of her own right makes herself active, or has her appearances on sufferance and is forced to draw in her sails, or is inactive and mute and pent within narrow bounds, or is openly displayed, no matter what her condition is, she always does good.

Why, then, do you think that the example of one who lives in honorable retirement is of little value? Accordingly, the best course by far is to combine leisure with business, whenever chance obstacles or the condition of the state shall prevent one's living a really active life; for a man is never so completely shut off from all pursuits that no opportunity is left for any honorable activity. Can you find any city more wretched than was that of the Athenians when it was being torn to pieces by the Thirty Tyrants? They had slain thirteen hundred citizens, all the best men, and were not for that reason ready to stop, but their very cruelty fed its own flame. In the city in which there was the Areopagus, a most god-fearing court, in which there was a senate and a popular assembly that was like a senate, there gathered together every day a sorry college of hangmen, and the unhappy senate-house was made too narrow by tyrants! Could that city ever find peace in which there were as many tyrants as there might be satellites? No hope even of recovering liberty could offer itself, nor did there seem to be room for any sort of help against such mighty strength of wicked men. For where could the wretched state find enough Harmodiuses?

Yet Socrates was in their midst and comforted the mourning city fathers, he encouraged those that were despairing of the state, reproached the rich men that were now dreading their wealth with a too late repentance of their perilous greed, while to those willing to imitate him he carried round with him a great example, as he moved a free man amid thirty masters. Yet this was the man that Athens herself murdered in prison, and Freedom herself could not endure the freedom of one who had mocked in security at a whole band of tyrants. And so you may learn both that the wise man has opportunity to display his power when the state is torn by trouble, and that effrontery, envy, and a thousand other cowardly vices hold sway when it is prosperous and happy. Therefore we shall either expand or contract our effort according as the state shall lend herself to us, according as Fortune shall permit us, but in any case we shall keep moving, and shall not be tied down and numbed by fear. Nay, he will be truly a man who, when perils are threatening from every side, when arms and chains are rattling around him, will neither endanger, nor conceal, his virtue; for saving oneself does not mean burying oneself.

Curius Dentatus said, truly as I think, that he would rather be a dead man than a live one dead;

for the worst of ills is to leave the number of the living before you die. But if you should happen upon a time when it is not at all easy to serve the state, your necessary course will be to claim more time for leisure and for letters, and, just as if you were making a perilous voyage, to put into harbor from time to time, and, without waiting for public affairs to release you, to separate yourself from them of your own accord. Our duty, however, will be, first, to examine our own selves, then, the matters that we shall undertake, and lastly, those for whose sake or in whose company we are undertaking them. Above all it is necessary for a man to estimate himself truly, because we commonly think that we can do more than we are able.

One man blunders by relying upon his eloquence, another makes more demand upon his fortune than it can stand, another burdens a weakly body with laborious tasks. Some men by reason of their modesty are quite unsuited to civil affairs, which need a strong front; some by reason of their stubborn pride are not fitted for court; some do not have their anger under control, and any sort of provocation hurries them to rash words; some do not know how to restrain their pleasantry and cannot abstain from dangerous wit. For all these retirement is more serviceable than employment; a headstrong and impatient nature should avoid all incitements to a freedom of speech that will prove harmful.

Next, we must estimate the matters themselves that we are undertaking, and must compare our strength with the things that we are about to attempt; for the doer must always be stronger than his task; burdens that are too heavy for their bearer must necessarily crush him. There are certain undertakings, moreover, that are not so much great as they are prolific, and thus lead to many fresh undertakings. Not only ought you to avoid those that give birth to new and multifarious employment, but you ought not to approach a task from which you are not free to retreat; you must put your hand to those that you can either finish, or at least hope to finish, leaving those untouched that grow bigger as you progress and do not cease at the point you intended.

And we must be particularly careful in our choice of men, and consider whether they are worthy of having us devote some part of our life to them, or whether the sacrifice of our time extends to theirs also; for certain people actually charge against us the services we do them. Athenodorus says that he would not go to dine with a man who would not feel indebted to him for doing so. You understand, I suppose, that much less would he go to dinner with those who recompense the services of friends by their table, who get down the courses of a meal as largesses, as if they were being intemperate to do honor to others. Take away the spectators and witnesses, and solitary gluttony will give them no pleasure.

But consider whether your nature is better adapted to active affairs or to leisurely study and contemplation, and you must turn towards that course to which the bent of your genius shall direct you. Isocrates laid hands upon Ephorus and led him away from the forum, thinking that he would be more useful in compiling the records of history; for inborn tendencies answer ill to compulsion, and where Nature opposes labor is in vain.

Nothing, however, gives the mind so much pleasure as fond and faithful friendship. What a blessing it is to have those to whose waiting hearts every secret may be committed with safety, whose knowledge of you you fear less than your knowledge of yourself, whose conversation soothes your anxiety, whose opinion assists your decision, whose cheerfulness scatters your sorrow, the very sight of whom gives you joy! We shall of course choose those who are free, as far as may be, from selfish desires; for vices spread unnoticed, and quickly pass to those nearest and do harm by their contact.

And so, just as in times of pestilence we must take care not to sit near those whose bodies are already infected and inflamed with disease, because we shall incur risks and be in danger from their very breath, so, in choosing our friends, we shall have regard for their character, so that we may appropriate those who are marked with fewest stains; to combine the sick with the sound is to spread disease. Yet I would not lay down the rule that you are to follow, or attach to yourself, none but a wise man. For where will you find him whom we have been seeking for so many centuries? In place of the best man take the one least bad! Opportunity for a happier choice scarcely could you have, were you searching for a good man among the Platos and the Xenophons and the rest of that glorious company of the Socratic breed, or, too, if you had at your command the age of Cato, which bore many men who were worthy to be born in Cato's time, just as it also bore many that were worse than had ever been known, and contrivers of the most monstrous crimes; for both classes were necessary in order that Cato might be understood — he needed to have good men that he might win their approval, and bad men that be might prove his strength.

But now, when there is such a great dearth of good men, you must be less squeamish in making your choice. Yet those are especially to be avoided who are melancholy and bewail everything, who find pleasure in every opportunity for complaint.

Though a man's loyalty and friendliness be assured, yet the companion who is always upset and bemoans everything is a foe to tranquillity.

Let us pass now to the matter of fortunes, which are the greatest source of human sorrow; for if you compare all the other ills from which we suffer: deaths, sicknesses, fears, longings, the endurance of pains and labors — with the evils which our money brings, this portion will far outweigh the other. And so we must reflect how much lighter is the sorrow of not having money than of losing it; and we shall understand that, the less poverty has to lose, the less chance it has to torment us. For you are wrong if you think that the rich suffer losses more cheerfully; the pain of a wound is the same in the largest and smallest bodies.

Bion says neatly that it hurts, the bald-head just as much as the thatched-head to have his hairs plucked. You may be sure that the same thing holds for the poor and the rich, that their suffering is just the same; for their money has a fast grip on both, and cannot be torn away without their feeling it. But, as I have said, it is more endurable and easier not to acquire it than to lose it, and therefore you will see that those whom Fortune has never regarded are more cheerful than those whom she has forsaken.

Diogenes, that high-souled man, saw this, and made it impossible for anything to be snatched from him. Do you call such a state poverty, want, need, give this security any disgraceful name you please. I shall not count the man happy, if you can find anyone else who has nothing to lose! Either I am deceived, or it is a regal thing to be the only one amid all the misers, the sharpers, the robbers, and plunderers who cannot be harmed. If anyone has any doubt about the happiness of Diogenes, he may likewise have doubt about the condition of the immortal gods as well — whether they are living quite unhappily because they have neither manors nor gardens nor costly estates farmed by a foreign tenant, nor a huge yield of interest in the forum.

All ye who bow down to riches, where is your shame? Come, turn your eyes upon heaven; you will see the gods quite needy, giving all and having nothing. Do you think that he who stripped himself of all the gilds of Fortune is a poor man or simply like the immortal gods? Would you say that Demetrius, the freedman of Pompey who was not ashamed to be richer than Pompey, was a happier man? He, to whom two underlings and a roomier cell would once have been wealth, used to have the number of his slaves reported to him every day as if he were the general of an army! But the only slave Diogenes had ran away from him once, and, when he was pointed out to him, he did not think it worth while to fetch him back. "It would be a shame," he said, "if Diogenes is not able to live without Manes, when Manes is able to live without Diogenes." But he seems to me to have cried: "Fortune, mind your own business; Diogenes has now nothing of yours. My slave has run away — nay, it is I that have got away free!"

A household of slaves requires clothes and food; so many bellies of creatures that are always hungry have to be filled, we have to buy clothing for them, and watch their most thievish hands, and use the services of people weeping and cursing. How much happier is he whose only obligation is to one whom he can most easily refuse himself! Since, however, we do not have such strength of character, we ought at least to reduce our possessions, so as to be less exposed to the injuries of Fortune.

In war those men are better fitted for service whose bodies can be squeezed into their armor than those whose bodies spill over, and whose very bulk everywhere exposes them to wounds. In the case of money, an amount that does not descend to poverty, and yet is not for removed from poverty, is the most desirable.

Moreover, we shall be content with this measure if we were previously content with thrift, without which no amount of wealth is sufficient, and no amount is not sufficiently ample, especially since the remedy is always near at hand, and poverty of itself is able to turn itself into riches by summoning economy. Let us form the habit of putting away from us mere pomp and of measuring the uses of things, not their decorative qualities. Let food subdue hunger, drink quench thirst; let lust follow the course of nature; let us learn to rely upon our limbs and to conform our dress and mode of life, not to the new fashions, but to the customs our ancestors approved; let us learn to increase our self-control, to restrain luxury, to moderate ambition, to soften anger, to view poverty with unprejudiced eyes, to cultivate frugality, even if many shall be ashamed, all the more to apply to the wants of nature the remedies that cost little, to keep unruly hopes and a mind that is intent upon the future, as it were, in chains, and to determine to seek our riches from ourselves rather than from Fortune.

It is never possible that all the diversity and injustice of mischance can be so repulsed, that many storms will not sweep down upon those who are spreading great sail. We must draw in our activities to a narrow compass in order that the darts of Fortune may fall into nothingness, and for this reason exiles and disasters have turned out to be benefits, and more serious ills have been healed by those that are lighter. When the mind is disobedient to precepts and cannot be restored by gentler means, why should it not be for its own good to have poverty, disgrace, and a violent overthrow of fortune applied to it — to match evil with evil? Let us then get accustomed to being able to dine without the multitude, to being the slave of fewer slaves, to getting clothes for the purpose for which they were devised, and to living in narrower quarters. Not only in the race and the contests of the Circus, but also in the arena of life we must keep to the inner circle.

Even for studies, where expenditure is most honorable, it is justifiable only so long as it is kept within bounds. What is the use of having countless books and libraries, whose titles their owners can scarcely read through in a whole lifetime? The learner is, not instructed, but burdened by the mass of them, and it is much better to surrender yourself to a few authors than to wander through many. Forty thousand books were burned at Alexandria; let someone else praise this library as the most noble monument to the wealth of kings, as did Titus Livius, who says that it was the most distinguished achievement of the good taste and solicitude of kings. There was no "good taste" or "solicitude" about it, but only learned luxury — nay, not even "learned," since they had collected the books, not for the sake of learning, but to make a show, just as many who lack even a child's knowledge of letters use books, not as the tools of learning, but as decorations for the dining-room.

Therefore, let just as many books be acquired as are enough, but not for mere show.

"It is more respectable," you say, "to squander money on these than on Corinthian bronzes and on pictures." But excess in anything becomes a fault. What excuse have you to offer for a man who seeks to have bookcases of citrus-wood and ivory, who collects the works of unknown or discredited authors and sits yawning in the midst of so many thousand books, who gets most of his pleasure from the outsides of volumes and their titles? Consequently it is in the houses of the laziest men that you will see a full collection of orations and history with the boxes piled right up to the ceiling; for by now among cold baths and hot baths a library also is equipped as a necessary ornament of a great house. I would readily pardon these men if they were led astray by their excessive zeal for learning. But as it is, these collections of the works of sacred genius with all the portraits that adorn them are bought for show and a decoration of their walls.

But it may be that you have fallen upon some phase of life which is difficult, and that, before you are aware, your public or your private fortune has you fastened in a noose which you can neither burst nor untie. But reflect that it is only at first that prisoners are worried by the burdens and shackles upon their legs; later, when they have determined not to chafe against them, but to endure them, necessity teaches them to bear them bravely, habit to bear them easily. In any sort of life you will find that there are amusements and relaxations and pleasures, if you are willing to consider your evils lightly rather than to make them hateful. On no score has Nature more deserved our thanks, who, since she knew to what sorrows we were born, invented habit as an alleviation for disasters, and thus quickly accustoms us to the most serious ills. No one could endure adversity if, while it continued, it kept the same violence that its first blows had.

All of us are chained to Fortune. Some are bound by a loose and golden chain, others by a tight chain of baser metal; but what difference does it make? The same captivity holds all men in its toils, those who have bound others have also been bound — unless perhaps you think that a chain on the left hand is a lighter one. Some are chained by public office, others by wealth; some carry the burden of high birth, some of low birth; some bow beneath another's empire, some beneath their own; some are kept in one place by exile, others by priesthoods. All life is a servitude. And so a man must become reconciled to his lot, must complain of it as little as possible, and must lay hold of whatever good it may have; no state is so bitter that a calm mind cannot find in it some consolation. Even small spaces by skillful planning often reveal many uses; and arrangement will make habitable a place of ever so small dimensions. Apply reason to difficulties; it is possible to soften what is hard, to widen what is narrow, and burdens will press less heavily upon those who bear them skillfully.

Moreover, we must not send our desires upon a distant quest, but we should permit them to have access to what is near, since they do not endure to be shut up altogether. Leaving those things that either cannot be done, or can be done only with difficulty, let us pursue what lies near at hand and allures our hope, but let us be aware that they all are equally trivial, diverse outwardly in appearance, within alike vain. And let us not envy those who stand in higher places; where there appeared heights, there are precipices. Those, on the other hand, whom an unkind lot has placed in a critical position, will be safer by reducing their pride in the things that are in themselves proud and lowering their fortune, so far as they shall be able, to the common level. While there are many who must necessarily cling to their pinnacle, from which they cannot descend without falling, yet they may bear witness that their greatest burden is the very fact that they are forced to be burdensome to others, being not lifted, but nailed on high.

By justice, by kindness, by courtesy, and by lavish and kindly giving let them prepare many safeguards against later mishaps, in hope whereof they may be more easy in their suspense. Yet nothing can free us from these mental waverings so effectively as always to establish some limit to advancement and not leave to Fortune the decision of when it shall end, but halt of our own accord far short of the limit that the examples of others urge. In this way there will be some desires to prick on the mind, and yet, because bounds have been set to them, they will not lead it to that which is unlimited and uncertain.

These remarks of mine apply, not to the wise man, but to those who are not yet perfect, to the mediocre, and to the unsound.

The wise man does not need to walk timidly and cautiously; for so great is his confidence in himself that he does not hesitate to go against Fortune, and will never retreat before her. Nor has he any reason to fear her, for he counts not merely his chattels and his possessions and his position, but even his body and his eyes and his hand and all else that makes life very dear to a man, nay, even himself, among the things that are given on sufferance, and he lives as one who has been lent to himself and will return everything without sorrow when it is reclaimed. Nor is he therefore cheap in his own eyes, because be knows that he does not belong to himself, but he will perform all his duties as diligently and as circumspectly as a devout and holy man is wont to guard the property entrusted to his protection.

When, however, he is bidden to give them up, he will not quarrel with Fortune, but will say: "I give thanks for what I have possessed and held. I have managed your property to great advantage, but, since you order me, I give it up, I surrender it gratefully and gladly. If you still wish me to have anything of yours, I shall guard it; if your pleasure is otherwise, I give back and restore to you my silver both wrought and coined, my house, and my household." Should Nature recall what she previously entrusted us with, we shall say to her also: "Take back the spirit that is better than when you gave it. I do not quibble or hang back; of my own free will I am ready for you to take what you gave me before I was conscious — away with it!"

What hardship is there in returning to the place from which you came? That man will live ill who will not know how to die well. Therefore we must take from the value we set upon this thing, and the breath of life must be counted as a cheap matter. As Cicero says we feel hostility to gladiators if they are eager to save their life no matter how; if they display contempt for it, we favor them. The same thing, you may know, applies to us; for often the cause of death is the fear of dying. Mistress Fortune, who uses us for her sport, says: "Why should I save you, you base and cowardly creature? You will be hacked and pierced with all the more wounds, because you do not know how to offer your throat. But you, who receive the steel courageously and do not withdraw your neck or put out your hands to stop it, shall both live longer and die more easily."

He who fears death will never do anything worthy of a man who is alive, but be who knows that these were the terms drawn up for him at the moment of his conception will live according to the bond, and at the same time will also with like strength of mind guarantee that none of the things that happen shall be unexpected. For by looking forward to whatever can happen as though it would happen, he will soften the attacks of all ills, which bring nothing strange to those who have been prepared beforehand and are expecting them; it is the unconcerned and those that expect nothing but good fortune upon whom they fall heavily. Sickness comes, captivity, disaster, conflagration, but none of them is unexpected — I always knew in what disorderly company Nature had confined me.

Many times has wailing for the dead been heard in my neighborhood; many times have the torch and the taper led untimely funerals past my threshold; often has the crash of a falling building resounded at my side; many of those whom the forum, the senate-house and conversation had bound to me a night has carried off, and the hands that were joined in friendship have been sundered by the grave. Should I be surprised if the dangers that always have wandered about me should at some time reach me? The number of men that will plan a voyage without thinking of storms is very great. I shall never be ashamed to quote a bad author if what he says is good. Publilius, who, whenever he abandoned the absurdities of farce and language directed to the gallery, had more vigor than the writers of comedy and tragedy, among many other utterances more striking than any that came from the buskined — to say nothing of the comic curtain's — stage, has also this:

Whatever can one man befall can happen just as well to all.

If a man lets this sink deep into his heart, and, when he looks upon the evils of others, of which there is a huge supply every day, remembers that they are free to come to him also, he will arm himself against them long before they attack him. It is too late to equip the soul to endure dangers after the dangers have arisen. You say: "I did not think this would happen," and "Would you have believed that this would happen?" But why not? Where are the riches that do not have poverty and hunger and beggary following close behind? What rank is there whose bordered robe and augur's wand and patrician boot-laces do not carry in their train rags and branded disgrace — a thousand stigmas and utter disrepute?

What kingdom is there for which ruin and a trampling underfoot and the tyrant and the hangman are not in store? Nor are such things cut off by long intervals, but between the throne and bending at another's knees there is but an hour's space. Know, then, that every lot in life is changeable, and that whatever befalls, any man can befall you also. You are rich: but are you any richer than Pompey? Yet he lacked even bread and water when Gaius, an old kinsman but a new sort of host, had opened to him the house of Caesar in order that he might have a chance to close his own! Though he owned so many rivers that had their source within his own lands and their mouth within his own lands, he had to beg for drops of water. In the palace of his kinsman he perished from hunger and thirst, and, while he was starving, his heir was arranging to give him a state funeral!

You have held the highest offices; but have you held any as great, as unlooked for, as comprehensive as those of Sejanus? Yet on the day on which the senate played the escort the people tore him to pieces! Of the man who had had heaped upon him all that gods and men were able to bestow nothing was left for the executioner to drag to the river! You are a king: it will not be Croesus to whom I shall direct you, who lived to see his own pyre both lighted and extinguished, who was forced to survive, not his kingdom only, but even his own death, nor Jugurtha, whom the Roman people gazed upon as a captive in less than a year after he had made them afraid. We ourselves have seen Ptolemy, king of Africa, and Mithridates, king of Armenia, under the charge of Gaius's guards; the one was sent into exile, the other was anxious to be sent there in better faith!

In view of this great mutability of fortune, that moves now upward, now downward, unless you consider that whatever can happen is likely to happen to you, you surrender yourself into the power of adversity, which any man can crush if he sees her first.

Our next concern will be not to labor either for useless ends or uselessly, that is, not to desire either what we are not able to accomplish, or what, if attained, will cause us to understand too late and after much shame the emptiness of our desires. In other words, neither should our labor be in vain and without result, nor the result unworthy of our labor; for as a rule sadness attends upon it, if there has been either lack of success or shame for success. We must curtail the restlessness that a great many men show in wandering through houses and theatres and forums; they thrust themselves into the affairs of others, and always appear to be busily engaged. If you ask one of these as he comes out of the house: "Where are you going? What have you in mind?" he will reply to you: "Upon my word, I really do not know; but I shall see some people, I shall do something."

They wander without any plan looking for employment, and they do, not what they have determined to do, but whatever they have stumbled upon. Their course is is aimless and idle as that of ants crawling among bushes, which idly bustle to the top of a twig and then to the bottom; many men are like these in their way of life, which one may not unjustly call "busy idleness." When you see some of them running as if they were going to a fire, you will be sorry for them; so often do they collide with those they meet and send themselves and others sprawling, though all the while they have been rushing to pay a call to someone who will not return it, or to attend the funeral of a man they do not know, or the trial of someone who is always having a suit, or the betrothal of some woman who is always getting married, and, having attached themselves to some litter, have in some places even carried it. Afterwards, when they are returning home wearied to no purpose, they swear that they themselves do not know why they left home, or where they have been, and, on the next day they will wander over the selfsame track. And so let all your effort be directed toward some object, let it keep some object in view!

It is not activity that makes men restless, but false conceptions of things render them mad. For even madmen do not become agitated without some hope; they are excited by the mere appearance of some object, the falsity of which is not apparent to their afflicted mind. In the same way every one of those who go forth to swell the throng is led around the city by worthless and trivial reasons; dawn drives a man forth though he has no task to do, and, after he has been crushed in many men's door-ways, all in vain, and has saluted their nomenclators one after another, and has been shut out by many, he finds that, of them all, not one is more difficult to catch at home than himself. From this evil is derived that most disgusting vice of eavesdropping and prying into public and secret matters and learning of many things that it is neither safe to tell nor safe to listen to.

I fancy that Democritus was thinking of this when he began: "If a man shall wish to live tranquilly, let him not engage in many affairs either public or private," referring of course to useless affairs. For if necessity demands, we must engage in many, even countless, affairs both public and private; but when there is no call from sacred duty, we must restrain other activities. For if a man engages in many affairs, he often puts himself in the power of Fortune, while his safest course is rarely to tempt her, always to be mindful of her, and never to put any trust in her promises. Say, "I will set sail unless something happens," and "I shall become praetor unless something hinders me," and "My enterprise will be successful unless something interferes."

This is why we say that nothing happens to a wise man contrary to his expectations — we release him, not from the accidents, but from the blunders of mankind, nor do all things turn out as he has wished, but as he has thought; but his first thought has been that something might obstruct his plans. Then, too, the suffering that comes to the mind from the abandonment of desire must necessarily be much lighter if you have not certainly promised it success. We ought also to make ourselves adaptable lest we become too fond of the plans we have formed, and we should pass readily to the condition to which chance has led us, and not dread shifting either purpose or positions — provided that fickleness, a vice most hostile to repose, does not get hold of us. For obstinacy, from which Fortune often wrests some concession, must needs be anxious and unhappy, and much more grievous must be a fickleness that nowhere shows self-restraint.

Both are foes to tranquillity — both the inability to change and the inability to endure. Most of all, the mind must be withdrawn from external interests into itself. Let it have confidence in itself, rejoice in itself, let it admire its own things, let it retire as far as possible from the things of others and devote itself to itself, let it not feel losses, let it interpret kindly even adversities.

Zeno, our master, when he received news of a shipwreck and heard that all his property had been sunk, said: "Fortune bids me to follow philosophy with fewer encumbrances." A tyrant was threatening the philosopher Theodorus with death and even with lack of burial: "You have the right," he replied, "to please yourself, you have within your power only a half pint of my blood; for as to burial, you are a fool if you think it makes any difference to me whether I rot above ground or beneath it." Julius Canus, a rarely great man, whom even the fact that he was born in our own age does not prevent our admiring, had had a long dispute with Gaius, and when, as he was leaving, Phalaris said to him: "That you may not by any chance comfort yourself with a foolish hope, I have ordered you to be executed," he replied: "Most excellent prince, I tender you my thanks."

I am not sure what he meant, for many explanations occur to me. Did he wish to be insulting and show him how great his cruelty must be if it made death a kindness? Or was he taunting him with the everyday proofs of insanity? — for those whose children had been murdered and whose property had been confiscated used to thank him — or was it that he accepted death as a happy escape? However it may be, it was a high-souled reply. But someone will say: "There was a possibility that after this Gaius might order him to live." Canus had no fear of that; it was well known that in orders of this sort Gaius was a man of his word! Will you believe that Canus spent the ten intervening days before his execution in no anxiety of any sort? What the man said, what he did, how tranquil he was, passes all credence.

He was playing chess when the centurion who was dragging off a whole company of victims to death ordered that he also be summoned. Having been called, he counted the pawns and said to his partner: "See that after my death you do not claim falsely that you won"; then nodding to the centurion, he said: "You will bear witness that I am one pawn ahead." Do you think that at that board Canus was playing a game? Nay, he was making game! His friends were sad at the thought of losing such a man; but "Why," said he, "are you sorrowful? You are wondering whether our souls are immortal; but I shall soon know." Nor up to the very end did he cease to search for truth and to make his own death a subject for debate.

His own teacher of philosophy was accompanying him, and, when they were not far from the low hill on which the daily sacrifice to Caesar, our god, was made, said: "What are you thinking of now, Canus, or what state of mind are you in?" And

Canus said: "I have determined to watch whether the spirit will be conscious that it is leaving the body when that fleetest of moments comes," and he promised that, if he discovered anything, he would make the round of his friends, and reveal to them what the state of the soul really is. Here is tranquillity in the very midst of the storm, here is a mind worthy of immortality — a spirit that summons its own fate to the proof of truth, that, in the very act of taking that one last step, questions the departing soul, and learns, not merely up to the point of death, but seeks to learn something even from death itself. No one has ever played the philosopher longer. Not hastily shall so great a man be abandoned, and he must be spoken of with respect. O most glorious soul, chief victim of the murders of Gaius, to the memory of all time will I consign thee!

But it does no good to have got rid of the causes of individual sorrow; for one is sometimes seized by hatred of the whole human race. When you reflect how rare is simplicity, how unknown is innocence, and how good faith scarcely exists, except when it is profitable, and when you think of all the throng of successful crimes and of the gains and losses of lust, both equally hateful, and of ambition that, so far from restraining itself within its own bounds, now gets glory from baseness — when we remember these things, the mind is plunged into night, and as though the virtues, which it is now neither possible to expect nor profitable to possess, had been overthrown, there comes overwhelming gloom.

We ought, therefore, to bring ourselves to believe that all the vices of the crowd are, not hateful, but ridiculous, and to imitate Democritus rather than Heraclitus. For the latter, whenever he went forth into public, used to weep, the former to laugh; to the one all human doings seemed to be miseries, to the other follies. And so we ought to adopt a lighter view of things, and put up with them in an indulgent spirit; it is more human to laugh at life than to lament over it. Add, too, that he deserves better of the human race also who laughs at it than he who bemoans it; for the one allows it some measure of good hope, while the other foolishly weeps over things that he despairs of seeing corrected.

And, considering everything, he shows a greater mind who does not restrain his laughter than he who does not restrain his tears, since the laugher gives expression to the mildest of the emotions, and deems that there is nothing important, nothing serious, nor wretched either, in the whole outfit of life. Let a man set before himself the causes, one by one, that give rise to joy and sadness, and he will learn that what Bion said is true, that all the doings of men are just like their beginnings, and that their life is no more respectable or serious than their conception, that born from nothingness they go back to nothingness.

Yet it is better to accept calmly the ways of the public and the vices of man, and be thrown neither into laughter nor into tears; for it is unending misery to be worried by the misfortunes of others, and unhuman pleasure to take delight in the misfortunes of ethers, just as it is a useless show of humanity to weep and pull a long face because someone is burying a son. In the matter of one's own misfortunes, too, the right way to act is to bestow on them the measure of sorrow that Nature, not custom, demands; for many shed tears in order to make a show of them, and, whenever a spectator is lacking, their eyes are dry, though they judge it disgraceful not to weep when everyone is doing it. This evil of depending on the opinion of others has become so deeply implanted that even grief, the most natural thing in the world, becomes now a matter of pretence.

I come now to a class of cases which is wont with good cause to sadden and bring us concern. When good men come to bad ends, when Socrates is forced to die in prison, Rutilius to live in exile, Pompey and Cicero to offer their necks to their own clients, and great Cato, the living image of all the virtues, by falling upon his sword to show that the end had come for himself and for the state at the same time, we needs must be distressed that

Fortune pays her rewards so unjustly. And what hope can anyone then have for himself when he sees that the best men suffer the worst fate?

What then is the answer? See the manner in which each one of them bore his fate, and if they were brave, desire with your heart hearts like theirs, if they perished like a woman and a coward, then nothing perished; either they deserve that you should admire their virtue, or they do not deserve that you should desire their cowardice. For if the greatest men by dying bravely make others cowards, what could be more shameful? Let us praise those deserving of praise over and over and say: "The braver a man is, the happier he is! You may escaped from all accident, jealousy, and sickness; you have gone forth from prison; it was not that you seemed to the gods to be worthy of evil fortune, but unworthy of being subject any longer to the power of Fortune." But those who draw back and on the very threshold of death look back toward life — there is need to lay hands on these!

I shall weep for no one who is happy, for no one who weeps; the one with his own hand has wiped away my tears, the other by his tears has made himself unworthy of having any of mine. Should I weep for Hercules because he was burned alive? or for Regulus because he was pierced by so many nails? or for Cato because he wounded his own wounds? All these by a slight sacrifice of time found out how they might become eternal, and by dying reached immortality.

And this, too, affords no small occasion for anxieties — if you are bent on assuming a pose and never reveal yourself to anyone frankly, in the fashion of many who live a false life that is all made up for show; for it is torturous to be constantly watching oneself and be fearful of being caught out of our usual role. And we are never free from concern if we think that every time anyone looks at us he is always taking-our measure; for many things happen that strip off our pretence against our will, and, though all this attention to self is successful, yet the life of those who live under a mask cannot be happy and without anxiety. But how much pleasure there is in simplicity that is pure, in itself unadorned, and veils no part of its character! Yet even such a life as this does run some risk of scorn, if everything lies open to everybody; for there are those who disdain whatever has become too familiar. But neither does virtue run any risk of being despised when she is brought close to the eyes, and it is better to be scorned by reason of simplicity than tortured by perpetual pretence. Yet we should employ moderation in the matter; there is much difference between living naturally and living carelessly.

Moreover, we ought to retire into ourselves very often; for intercourse with those of dissimilar natures disturbs our settled calm, and rouses the passions anew, and aggravates any weakness in the mind that has not been thoroughly healed. Nevertheless the two things must be combined and resorted to alternately — solitude and the crowd. The one will make us long for men, the other for ourselves, and the one will relieve the other; solitude will cure our aversion to the throng, the throng our weariness of solitude. And the mind must not be kept invariably at the same tension, but must be diverted to amusements.

Socrates did not blush to play with little children, and Cato, when he was wearied by the cares of state, would relax his mind with wine, and Scipio would disport his triumphal and soldierly person to the sound of music, moving not with the voluptuous contortions that are now the fashion, when men even in walking squirm with more than a woman's voluptuousness, but in the manly style in which men in the days of old were wont to dance during the times of sport and festival, risking no loss of dignity even if their own enemies looked on. The mind must be given relaxation; it will arise better and keener after resting. As rich fields must not be forced — for their productiveness, if they have no rest, will quickly exhaust them — so constant labor will break the vigor of the mind, but if it is released and relaxed a little while, it will recover its powers; continuous mental toil breeds in the mind a certain dullness and languor.

Nor would the desire of men tend so much in this direction unless sport and amusement brought a sort of pleasure that was natural, but the frequent use of these will steal all weight and all force from the mind; for sleep also is necessary for refreshment, nevertheless if you prolong it throughout the day and night, it will be death. There is a great difference between slackening and removing your bond! The founders of our laws appointed days of festival in order that men might be forced by the state into merry-making, thinking that it was necessary to modify their toil by some interruption of their tasks; and among great men, as I have remarked, some used to set aside fixed days every month for a holiday, some divided every day into play-time and work-time.

Asinius Pollio, the great orator, I remember, had such a rule, and never worked at anything beyond the tenth hour; he would not even read letters after that hour for fear something new might arise that needed attention, but in those two hours laid aside the weariness of the whole long day. Some break off in the middle of the day, and reserve some task that requires lighter effort for the afternoon hours. Our ancestors, too forbade any new motion to be made in the senate after the tenth hour. The soldier divides his watches, and those who have just returned from an expedition have the whole night free.

We must be indulgent to the mind, and from time to time must grant it the leisure that serves as its food and strength. And, too, we ought to take walks out-of-doors in order that the mind may be strengthened and refreshed by the open air and much breathing; sometimes it will get new vigor from a journey by carriage and a change of place and festive company and generous drinking. At times we ought to reach the point even of intoxication, not drowning ourselves in drink, yet succumbing to it; for it washes away troubles, and stirs the mind from its very depths and heals its sorrow just as it does certain ills of the body; and the inventor of wine is not called the Releaser on account of the license it gives to the tongue, but because it frees the mind from bondage to cares and emancipates it and gives it new life, and makes it bolder in all that it attempts. But, as in freedom, so in wine there is a wholesome moderation.

It is believed that Solon and Arcesilaus were fond of wine, and Cato has been reproached for drunkenness; but whoever reproaches that man will more easily make reproach honorable than Cato base. Yet we ought not to do this often, for fear that the mind may contract an evil habit, nevertheless there are times when it must be drawn into rejoicing and freedom, and gloomy sobriety must be banished for a while. For whether we believe with the Greek poet that "sometimes it is a pleasure also to rave," or with Plato that "the sane mind knocks in vain at the door of poetry," or with Aristotle that "no great genius has ever existed without some touch of madness" — be that as it may, the lofty utterance that rises above the attempts of others is impossible unless the mind is excited.

When it has scorned the vulgar and the commonplace, and has soared far aloft fired by divine inspiration, then alone it chants a strain too lofty for mortal lips. So long as it is left to itself, it is impossible for it to reach any sublime and difficult height; it must forsake the common track and be driven to frenzy and champ the bit and run away with its rider and rush to a height that it would have feared to climb by itself. Here are the rules, my dearest Serenus, by which you may preserve tranquillity, by which you may restore it, by which you may resist the vices that steal upon it unawares. Yet be sure of this — none of them is strong enough to guard a thing so frail unless we surround the wavering mind with earnest and unceasing care.

Made in the USA
Coppell, TX
24 December 2020